Нашедший подкову

Whoever Has Found a Horseshoe

Osip Mandelstam

Whoever Has Found a Horseshoe

(A Pindaric fragment)

Centenary Presentation

Moscow

1923

Translated from the Russian by
Anthony Barnett

Drawings by
Lucy Rose Cunningham

A·B

Lewes

2023

Osip Mandelstam
Whoever Has Found a Horseshoe
is a translation of
Нашедший подкову
Nashedshiy podkovu
first published in
Красная ночь
Krasnaya noch´ [Red Night], no. 2
Moscow, March–April 1923

Translation, Afterword Copyright © Anthony Barnett 2022, 2023
Drawings Copyright © Lucy Rose Cunningham 2022, 2023

Anthony Barnett is hereby identified as the moral rights
holder of the translation in this version of the work and
Lucy Rose Cunningham of the drawings in this work

Frontispiece
Osip Mandelstam, a suburb of Paris, 1907 or 1908
archive Ye. E. Mandelstam

Thank you Lucy Rose Cunningham, and
Caroline Clark, Timothy Harris, Timothy Holmes

Part of the proceeds from sales of this
book is given to TrueRussia.org

All rights reserved
reprinting or online posting in whole or in
part without the written permission of the
copyright holders is prohibited except
for short quotation as allowed in
fair use in such as a review

Typeset in Centaur MT with Russian in
after-Centaur Coelacanth by AB©omposer
Printed by CPI Group (UK) Ltd

First published 31 March 2023 by
Allardyce Book ABP
14 Mount Street · Lewes · East Sussex BN7 1HL [E]UK
www.abar.net

Distributed in USA by SPD
1341 Seventh Street · Berkeley CA 94710-1409
www.spdbooks.org

CIP records for this book are available from
The British Library and The Library of Congress

ISBN 978-0-907954-67-5

Whoever Has Found a Horseshoe

(A Pindaric fragment)

We may face the forest and say:
Here is a forest with ship masts and timbers:
The pink-tinged pines
Freed from the weight of their clumps to their crowns
Should groan in the gale
Like solitary stone pines
In furious unforested air.
The plumbline, fastened to the prancing deck, held in the wind's salt step.

And a seafarer,
Loosed in a thirst for space,
Draws a fragile sextant through waterlogged furrows,
To set the rough sea surface
To the earth's embrace.

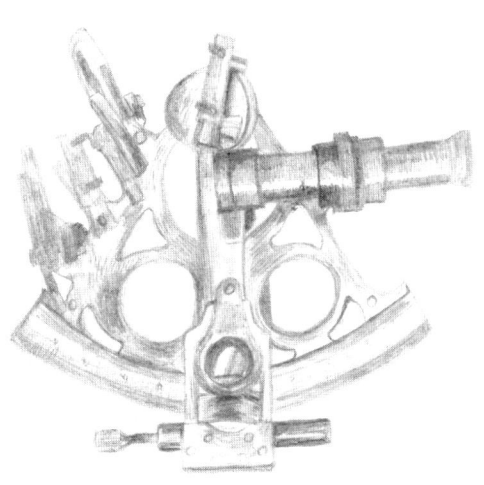

And breathing the smell of resinous tears
Weeping through planking,
Admiring the bulkhead
Arrangement of uprights riveted
Not by the calm Bethlehem carpenter,
But another—
              father of voyages,
                              seagoer's friend,
We say:
They also stood on the earth
Uncomfortable as an ass's back,
Their crowns oblivious to their roots,
Astride a famous mountain edge,
Braying in the fresh torrential rain,
Offering to the skies their palace goods in vain
For a pinch of salt.

Where shall we start?
Everything sways and splits,
Similes quiver in the air,
No one word better than another,
Metaphors drone in the earth,
And competing with the racetrack's snorting favourites
Light two-wheeled shays
Harnessed in show to laborious flocks
Fly apart.

Thrice blessed whoever enshrines a name in song,—
A song graced with a name
Outshines those that are not—
A fillet on its forehead distinguishes it among friends,
Forestalling unconsciousness with stupefying scents—
Be it male proximity,
Or the powerful scent of animal fur,
Or simply the fragrance of thyme, rubbed in the palms.

When the air
Is as dark as water everything living swims like a fish,
Pushing with fins through the sphere,
Dense, resilient,
A little warm—
A crystal wherein wheels rotate and horses shy,
Neaera's moist humus, newly turned up every night
By pitchforks,
           tridents,
                      mattocks
                                and ploughs.
The air worked over as thick as the earth:
You cannot get out, it's hard to get in.

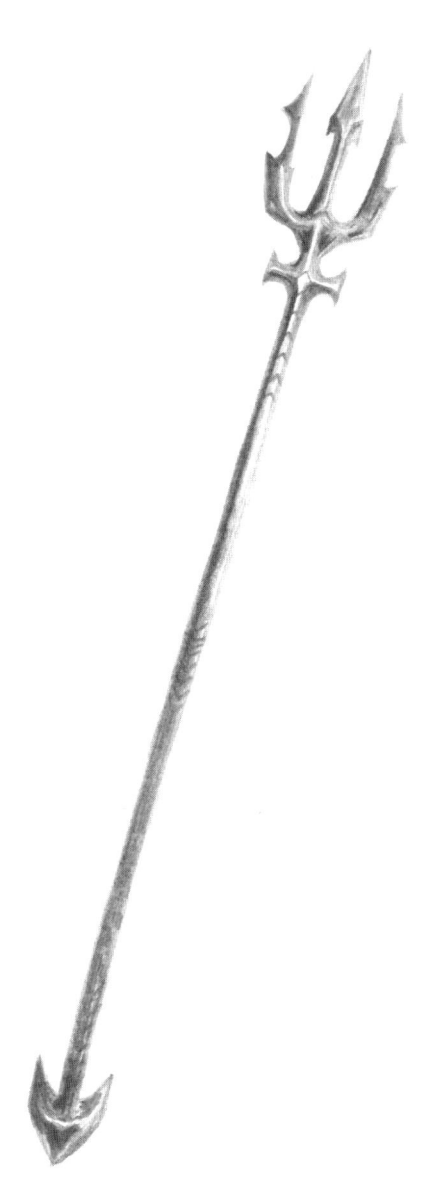

A verdant rustling bats through the trees.
Children play knucklebones with the vertebrae of animal dead.
Our years' fragile reckoning draws to a close.
My thanks for what was.
I myself was mistaken. I lost count.
The age rang like a golden globe,
Hollow,
      founded,
            standing free,
At every touch it answered "Yes" or "No",
The way a child talks:
"I'll give you an apple", "I won't give you an apple"—
Its face the perfect cast of the voice
That speaks these words.

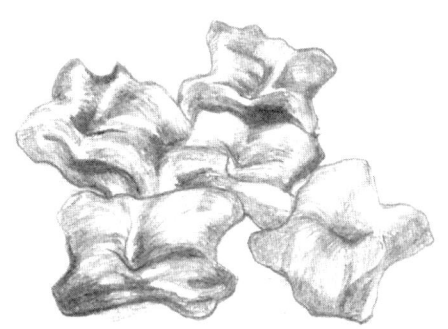

The sound rings on though the source has gone.
The stallion lies in the dust, in a lather, and snorts,
The neck's sharp curve
Recalls the race with legs outstretched,
When there weren't just four,
But as many as the road has stones,
Come alive by fours
As many as the leaps and bounds of blazing hooves.

So
Whoever has found a horseshoe blows away the dust,
Buffs it up with wool
Until it shines.
Then
Hangs it over the door,
To rest,
No striking sparks on flint again.
Human lips, with nothing more to say,
Keep the shape of the last word said,
And the hand still feels the weight,
Though the pitcher's
                splashed half empty
                                carrying it back to the house.

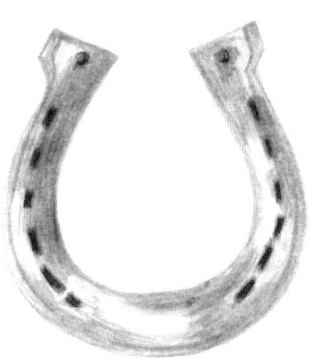

What I'm saying now
Isn't said by me,
It's dug up out of the ground
Like grains of petrified wheat.
Some
        depict a lion on their coins,
Others
        heads.
Assorted
Cakes of copper, gold and bronze
Lie in the earth, their honour the same.
The age,
A bit between its teeth,
Has left its mark.
Time clips me like a coin,
And already I'm not enough for myself . . .

                              Moscow, 1923

AFTERWORD

I first published a version of this translation in *PN Review*, issue 67, vol. 15, no. 5 (May–June 1989), a little differently titled. I had benefited from studying other translations, notably the literal version in Clarence Brown, *Mandelstam* (Cambridge University Press, 1973). With the assistance of native Russian speaker Marie Karp, I revised the translation for inclusion in a book about my work *The Poetry of Anthony Barnett*, ed. M. Grant (1993). I revised it yet again for inclusion in my collected *Translations* (Tears in the Fence, in assoc., Allardyce Book ABP, 2012). This fourth version, first published in *Long Poem Magazine*, no. 18 (Winter, 2017), benefits from close reading by Russian speaker and poet Caroline Clark who has pointed out, in particular, two errors ubiquitous in translations of this poem. The Russian original has two different words for "pines" (lines 3 and 6) and the second is "stone pines". In the last line of the fifth stanza, most translations, some surely taking their cue from Brown, have the herb "savory". In fact, the Russian is a regional word for "thyme", which at least one other translation does have. This makes perfect sense, not least because it is hard to detect, however much the herb is loved, a "fragrance" from "savory", even when "rubbed in the palms", though not hard from "thyme", and that is what at last led me to question "savory".

"Whoever Has Found a Horseshoe" is Mandelstam's only unrhymed poem in free verse. Yet there are a few moments here where rhyme came to me unforced. I have avoided the temptation, to which I succumbed in earlier versions, to write in the third stanza "mountain chain" in place of the correct "mountain ridge" (or "edge" as I have it, as in, for example, the Lake District's Striding Edge) and rhyme would be a bit forced were I to write "grain of salt" rather than "pinch of salt". Among other amendments, Mandelstam's initial caps at the beginning of each line are restored.

This version, unlike the earlier versions, is based on the text established in Osip Mandel´shtam: *Stikhotvoreniya, Proza* [Osip Mandelstam: *Poems, Prose*] (Moscow, Ripol Klassik, 2002), the main differences being punctuation and, in particular, lineation. Mandelstam made handwritten amendments to the poem's appearance in the journal *Krasnaya noch´* [*Red Night*], no. 2 (Moscow, March–April 1923), which are incorporated. This is, to my knowledge, the first translation to be based on the newly established text. In addition to corrections and amendments to vocabulary and phrasing, lineation and stanza breaks are in many places different.

I still cannot claim that my translation is finished though I am not displeased with this fourth state—or fifth, as, indeed, an "A" is added, in the sixth stanza, to read "A crystal"; and a line rewritten, in the seventh, in light of better understanding, viz. it is not the universal game of knucklebones later known as jacks that the children are playing but a Russian game, "babki", also translated "knucklebones", in which bones set in a row, or other standing disposition, are knocked over with a bat or a jetton.

Here, each strophe, of which there are ten, has been given its own page opposite a Lucy Rose Cunningham drawing. The drawings were made in May 2022.

A word about the orthography of Mandelstam's name: transcription is correct as Mandel´shtam, so to speak, but, as recorded in Brown, he himself asked that it be written Mandelstam.

AB, LEWES, JUNE 2022

OSIP MANDELSTAM
was born in Warsaw in 1891; he grew up in Saint Petersburg
and died in a Soviet transit camp near Vladivostok in 1938

Lucy Rose Cunningham is a poet and artist
who made the drawings for Anthony Barnett
Book Paradise: Spillikins